A New Tune A Day ™
for Flute

The useful addition of chord symbols for many of the pieces in this book
will enable the teacher to provide an accompaniment on guitar or piano.

D1118534

Boston Music Company
part of The Music Sales Group
London/New York/Paris/Sydney/Copenhagen/Berlin/Madrid/Tokyo

Foreword

Since its appearance in the early 1930s, C. Paul Herfurth's original *A Tune A Day* series has become the most popular instrumental teaching method of all time. Countless music students have been set on their path by the clear, familiar, proven material, and the logical, sensibly-paced progression through the lessons within the book.

The teacher will find that the new books have been meticulously rewritten by experienced teachers: instrumental techniques and practices have been updated and the musical content has been completely overhauled.

The student will find clearly-presented, uncluttered material, with familiar tunes and a gentle introduction to the theoretical aspects of music. The books are now accompanied by audio CDs of examples and backing tracks to help the student develop a sense of rhythm, intonation and performance at an early stage.

As in the original books, tests are given following every five lessons. Teachers are encouraged to present these as an opportunity to ensure that the student has a good overview of the information studied up to this point.

The following extract from the foreword to the original edition remains as true today as the day it was written:

The value of learning to count aloud from the very beginning cannot be over-estimated. Only in this way can a pupil sense rhythm. Rhythm, one of the most essential elements of music, and usually conspicuous by its absence in amateur ensemble playing, is emphasized throughout.

Eventual success in mastering the instrument depends on regular and careful application to its technical demands. Daily practice should not extend beyond the limits of the player's physical endurance — the aim should be the gradual development of tone control alongside assured finger-work.

Music-making is a lifelong pleasure, and at its heart is a solid understanding of the principles of sound production and music theory. These books are designed to accompany the student on these crucial first steps: the rewards for study and practice are immediate and lasting.

Welcome to the world of music!

Sincere thanks to Alison Hayhurst for her invaluable help with this book.

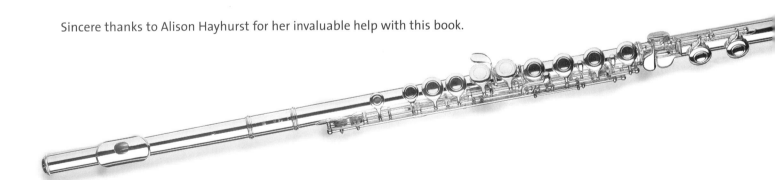

Published by
Boston Music Company

Exclusive Distributors:
Music Sales Corporation
257 Park Avenue South, New York, NY 10010, USA.
Music Sales Limited
8/9 Frith Street, London W1D 3JB, England.
Music Sales Pty Limited
120 Rothschild Avenue, Rosebery, NSW 2018, Australia.

This book © Copyright 2006 Boston Music Company,
a division of Music Sales Corporation

Edited by David Harrison
Music processed by Paul Ewers Music Design
Original compositions and arrangements by Ned Bennett
Cover and book designed by Chloë Alexander
Photography by Matthew Ward
Model: Sasha Haworth
Printed in the United States of America
 by Vicks Lithograph and Printing Corporation
Backing tracks by Guy Dagul
CD performance by Alison Hayhurst
CD recorded, mixed and mastered by Jonas Persson and John Rose

Your Guarantee of Quality

As publishers, we strive to produce every book to the highest commercial
standards. The music has been freshly engraved and the book has been
carefully designed to minimize awkward page turns and to make playing
from it a real pleasure. Throughout, the printing and binding have been
planned to ensure a sturdy, attractive publication which should give years
of enjoyment. If your copy fails to meet our high standards, please inform
us and we will gladly replace it.

www.musicsales.com

Contents

Rudiments of music

The staff

Music is written on a grid of five lines called a *staff*.
At the beginning of each staff is placed a special symbol called a *clef* to describe the approximate range of the instrument for which the music is written.

This example shows a *treble clef*, generally used for melody instruments.

The staff is divided into equal sections of time, called *bars* or *measures*, by *barlines*.

Note values

Different symbols are used to show the time value of *notes*, and each *note value* has an equivalent symbol for a rest, representing silence.

The **eighth note**, often used to signify a half beat, is written with a solid head and a stem with a tail. The eighth-note rest is also shown.

The **quarter note**, often used to signify one beat, is written with a solid head and a stem. The quarter-note rest is also shown.

The **half note** is worth two quarter notes. It is written with a hollow head and a stem. The half-note rest is placed on the middle line.

The **whole note** is worth two half notes. It is written with a hollow head. The whole-note rest hangs from the fourth line.

Other note values

Note values can be increased by half by adding a dot after the note head. Here a half note and quarter note are together worth a *dotted* half note.

Grouping eighth notes

Where two or more eighth notes follow each other, they can be joined by a *beam* from stem to stem.

Time signatures

The number of beats in a bar is determined by the *time signature*, a pair of numbers placed after the clef. The upper number shows how many beats each bar contains, while the lower number indicates what kind of note value is used to represent a single beat. This lower number is a fraction of a whole note, so that 4 represents quarter notes and 8 represents eighth notes.

C, for *common time*, is another way to write $\frac{4}{4}$.

6 means six eighth notes 8 to the bar.

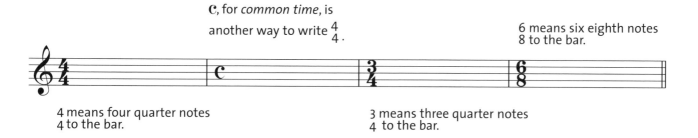

4 means four quarter notes 4 to the bar.

3 means three quarter notes 4 to the bar.

Note names

Notes are named after the first seven letters of the alphabet and are written on lines or spaces on the staff, according to pitch.

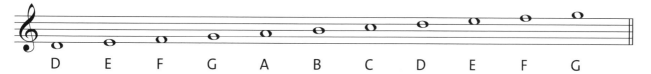

D E F G A B C D E F G

Accidentals

The pitch of a note can be altered up or down a half step (or *semitone*) by the use of sharp and flat symbols. These temporary pitch changes are known as *accidentals*.

The *sharp* (♯) raises the pitch of a note.   The *natural* (♮) returns the note to its original pitch.

The *flat* (♭) lowers the pitch of a note.

Ledger lines

Ledger lines are used to extend the range of the staff for low or high notes.

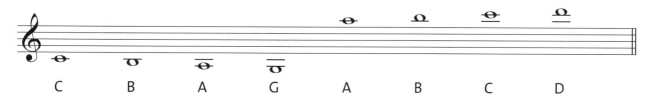

C B A G A B C D

Barlines

Various different types of barlines are used:

Double barlines divide one section of music from another.   *Final* barlines show the end of a piece of music.

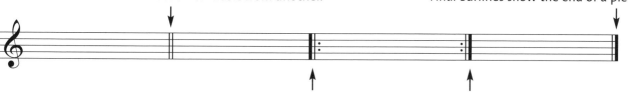

Repeat marks show a section to be repeated.

Before you play:

The flute and accessories Your complete flute outfit should include the following:

• Pull-through cleaning cloth

• Headjoint

• Footjoint

• Main body

• Cleaning duster

• Cleaning rod

Setting-up routine

1. Use a twisting action to push the footjoint gently onto the main body of the flute. Align the rod of the footjoint with the keys on the main body.

2. Again with a twisting action push the headjoint into the main body. Align the center of the lip hole with the center of the keys.

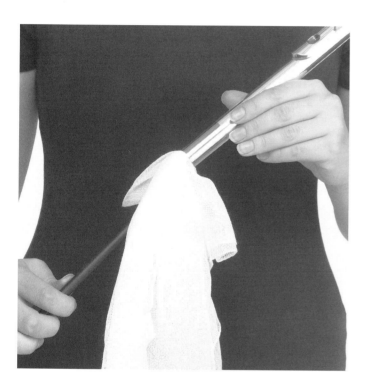

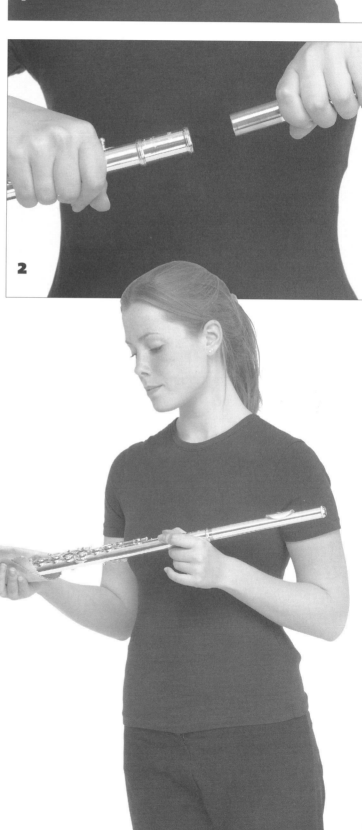

Important

Always dry your flute thoroughly after playing using the cleaning rod to push the cloth down inside the instrument. Make sure the rod is completely covered to prevent the risk of scratching the inside of the flute.

Don't keep the damp cloth in the case with your flute.
Never use polish to clean the outside of the flute; a soft, clean cloth is ideal.

goals:

1. **Breathing using the diaphragm**
2. **Formation of the mouth shape (embouchure)**
3. **Tonguing**
4. **Holding the flute**
5. **The notes B, A and G**
6. **Counting while playing; whole notes, half notes, and quarter notes**

Breathing

A relaxed, controlled posture is essential for comfort and correct breathing.

When breathing in and out, always use your diaphragm. This is a large membrane underneath your rib cage which causes your stomach to go *out* when breathing in and to go *in* when breathing out.

You will be able to control your breathing far more effectively using your diaphragm than if you were to breathe with the *intercostal* muscles high up in your chest.

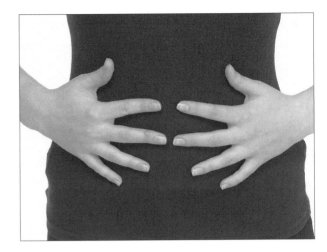

Exercise 1:

Breathe in counting four beats, then breathe out counting 4 and so on, always using the diaphragm and maintaining a steady flow of air.

In, 2, 3, 4,   Out, 2, 3, 4,   In...

Place one hand on your stomach to check whether it is going out as you breathe in then in when you breathe out.

Tonguing and embouchure

To produce your first sound, it is easiest to work with just the headjoint, so remove it from the rest of the flute. Say the word *too* and then say it again without engaging your vocal chords. Notice how your tongue acts as a valve that blocks the air flow until the desired moment.

Hold the head joint in front of your mouth with the open end to the right, and the mouth hole central to your lips. While keeping the mouth hole level, feel for the near edge of the hole with the bottom edge of your bottom lip. Press the headjoint on firmly. Your bottom lip should cover just a third of the hole.

Exercise 2: your first notes

Breathe in while setting the embouchure.

Play these four notes, tonguing each one and counting steadily throughout.

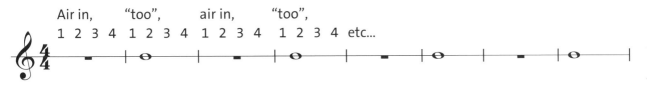

Air in,   "too",   air in,   "too",
1 2 3 4   1 2 3 4   1 2 3 4   1 2 3 4   etc...

Make sure the cheeks remain taught: don't puff them out.

Now reassemble the flute, hold it up without pressing any of the keys and repeat exercise 2.

Holding the flute

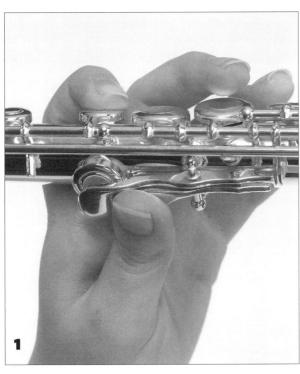

1

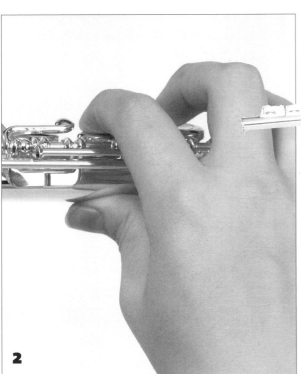

2

Position the top joint of your left thumb over the long *paddle-shaped* key at the back.

The flute rests on the lowest section of your index finger. Curl it around to the front, hugging the body of the flute.

Cover the keys as shown in picture 1.

Now place the tip of your right thumb underneath the flute beneath the third key from the bottom end of the main body.

Curl your fingers over the top and cover the lowest three circular keys of the main body as shown in picture 2.

Now push down the top key on the footjoint with your little finger.

The notes B, A and G

B

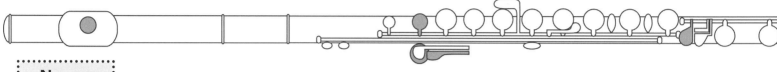

A

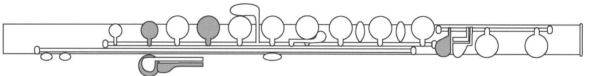

G

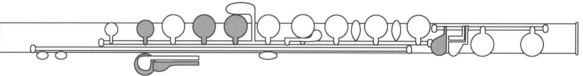

Exercise 3:

Breathe before the beginning of this exercise and in the rests.

Don't forget to tongue each note. A four-beat note is called a **whole note**.

Exercise 4:

Each of the notes and rests here are **half notes,** worth two beats.

Exercise 5:

These notes and rests are all **quarter notes,** worth one beat each. Breathe in quickly during quarter-note rests.

Pieces for Lesson 1

Valley Song

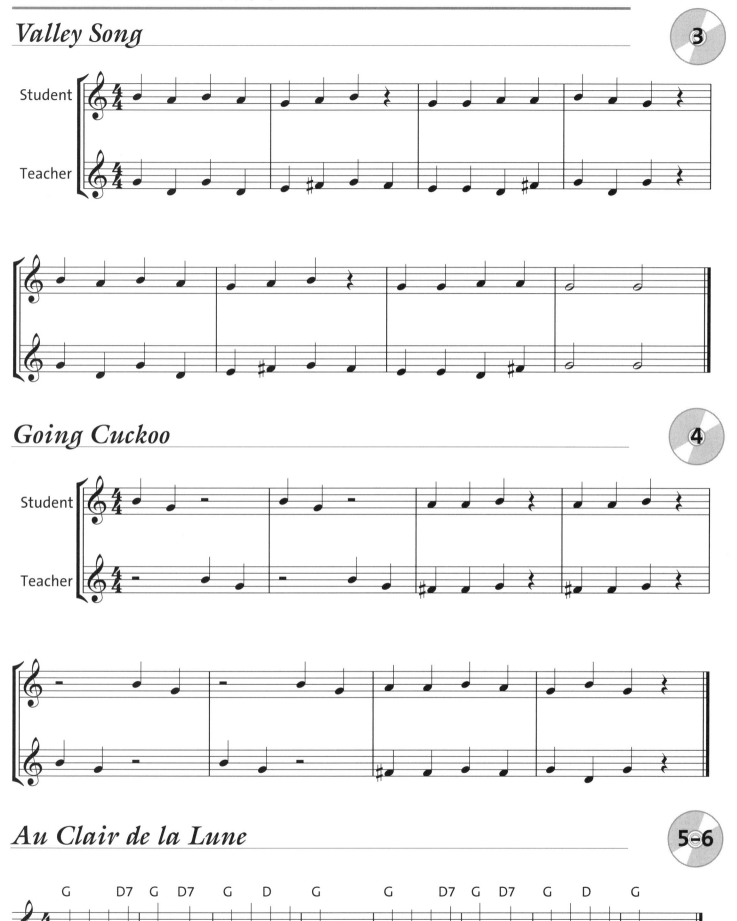

Going Cuckoo

Au Clair de la Lune

1. **The note C**
2. **Open throat breathing**
3. **Dotted half notes**
4. **Three beats in a bar**

The note C

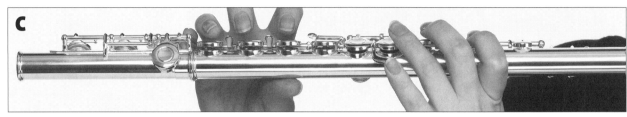

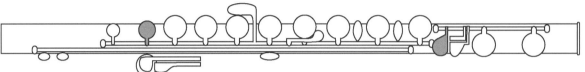

OPENING YOUR THROAT

Blow on the back of your hand. You will feel the air is cold.
Now try again, pretending that you are steaming up a window.
This time the air on the back of your hand should feel warm because you have just breathed out with your throat open. You should keep your throat open at all times when playing as it will improve your tone.

Stand with a relaxed posture, take a good deep breath and play the note with an open throat, using the diaphragm to control the air flow.

Exercise 1:

The symbol above this note is called a **pause** (or *fermata*). It means you should hold the note for longer than its actual value of four beats. Hold this one for as long as you can. Play with an **open throat**.

Long notes like this one should be the first thing you practice every day.

Exercise 2:

Play these notes in tempo with an open throat. The little commas are *breath marks*.

Take a very quick breath here without disrupting the 4-beat count.

Exercise 3:

The coordination of your fingers and your tongue is called *articulation*.

It is very important to develop this so all notes sound clean and precise.

Don't be satisfied with any untidiness!

Dotted notes

A dot placed to the right of a note multiplies its duration (value) by one and a half.

This means that a half note with a dot would increase in duration from two beats to three (2+1=3).

Count: 1   2   3   4   1   2   3   4

Exercise 4:

Count carefully as you play these notes. Remember the open throat.

Time signatures

So far all the exercises and pieces have had a **time signature** of four beats to every bar:

1, 2 , 3 , 4 , **1**, 2 , 3 , 4 , **1**, 2 , 3 , 4 etc.

Many pieces, however, contain three beats per bar.

This means that the count in your head will be **1** , 2 , 3 , **1** , 2 , 3 , **1** , 2 , 3 etc.

A waltz is a dance that uses this time signature.

Exercise 5:

Count three beats per bar, as shown by the top number of the time signature, and make sure you don't get confused between notes in spaces (A and C) and notes on lines (G and B).

Count: 1 2 3   1 2 3   1 2 3

THINK!

Are you still relaxed when you play? Remember to keep your shoulders down and breathe using your diaphragm.

Check that your bottom lip is in the correct position when you play, and that your right little finger is always pushing its key down.

13

Pieces for Lesson 2

7-8 *Back To Bed*

9 *Grumpy Graham*

Student
Teacher

10 *Medieval Dance*

Student
Teacher

11 *Barcarolle*

Offenbach

Student
Teacher

goals:

1. **The notes F and B flat (B♭)**
2. **Tones and semitones**
3. **Tied notes**
4. **The key of F major**

The notes F and B♭

F

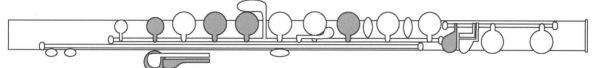

B♭

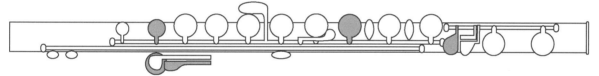

Exercise 1:

Play this one a few times, holding the note for as long as is comfortable.

Exercise 2: tones and semitones

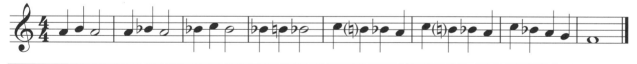

The difference in pitch between A and B is called a tone.
A to B♭ is only a semitone, and B♭ to B is also a semitone.
A semitone is the smallest interval that can be played on most instruments.

Exercise 3:

Play this one many times to ensure that your tongue, fingers and thumb (if needed) all move together.

Exercise 4:

Don't get confused between F, A, and C, which all look a bit similar.

Ties and tied notes

Two notes of the same pitch can be joined together to make a longer note by *tying* them together.
A curved line is drawn from one to the other to show this. The note is then held for the *combined value*
of the two notes. This is usually needed if a note needs to carry into the next bar.

Here are some examples:

is held for **3** beats   is held for **6** beats

Exercise 5:

Count very carefully here.

Count: **1**   **2**   **3**   **4**   **1**   **2...**

Different keys

If you try to sing a simple tune such as *The Star Spangled Banner*, you may find early on that you can't reach
the high notes without really straining. The solution is to start the piece a little lower. This time, you may be
able to sing the high notes perfectly. You are now singing the piece in a different *key*.

There are many different keys in music, each of which needs its own set of notes.
The key of C major is easy as it requires only natural notes. The key of F major requires all Bs to be B♭.
The key of a piece is shown by a *key signature*.

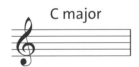

Notice that exercises 3 and 5 require B♭ instead of B, and that they begin and end on the note F.
They are all in the key of F major.

Exercise 6: reading music with a key signature

You must play all Bs as B♭s.

Exercise 7: comparing music in two different keys

The first is in G major (don't worry about the the sharp symbol in the key signature, you won't need it).
The second is in F major.

Pieces for Lesson 3

Jingle Bells

Largo (from the *New World Symphony*)

Dvořák

Lightly Row

Student

Teacher

Knight Time

Lesson 4

goals:

1. **The note D in the middle register**
2. **Dynamics (loud and soft)**
3. **Slurred notes**

The note D

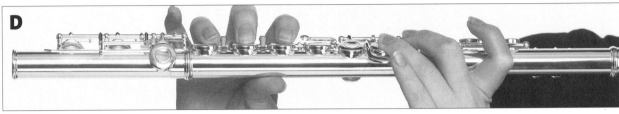

Try to make a slightly smaller hole between your lips and push your bottom lip forward a fraction.
You must also remove your right little finger.

Exercise 1:

Hold each note for a full breath. Breathe between each one.

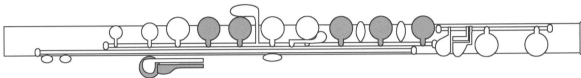

Exercise 2: fiddling fingers

Practice this very slowly to begin with, and build up the speed until all the fingerings become automatic.

Exercise 3: moving by step and by *leap* in two keys

Dynamics

Notes and rhythms are two of the elements of music, but without expression, music can be lifeless and mechanical. One of the obvious ways of introducing *color* into music is to play sections of pieces or phrases at different levels of loudness.

f stands for the word *forte* and means loud.   *p* stands for the word *piano* and means quiet.

Exercise 4:

Play these notes according to the dynamic displayed underneath.
Use your diaphragm to increase the airflow for the loud notes, and decrease the airflow for the quiet ones.

18

Slurs

In all the pieces and exercises so far you have tongued every note, that is, you have started each note with a *t* as in *too*. This can make the music sound a bit disjointed, and spoils the flow of gentle pieces such as *Barcarolle* in lesson 2.

Music is made smoother by slurring notes together. This means you should only tongue the first note of the slur. All other notes included in the slur are played by just changing the fingering.

Slurs are shown by lines which look like ties, but the notes will be of different pitches.

Exercise 5: slurred pairs

Only tongue the first of each pair of notes, but keep the air flowing as you play the second.

Exercise 6:

You must slur three notes at a time here. The steady **1**, 2, 3 count is unaffected by slurs.

Exercise 7:

Try *Barcarolle* again with slurs and with the dynamic shown. It should sound much more like a lullaby.

Pieces for Lesson 4

19-20 *When The Saints Go Marching In*

21-22 *Joshua Fought The Battle Of Jericho*   Spiritual

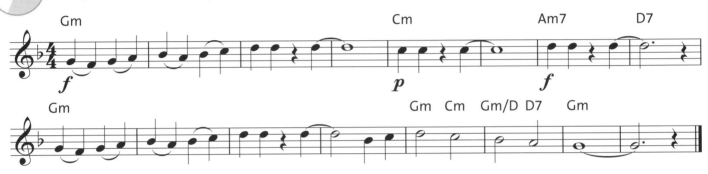

23-24 *Coventry Carol* (adapted)

Canon For Two

The second player starts one bar behind the first player.

goals:

1. **The note E, and F in the middle register**
2. **Octaves**
3. **The F major scale**
4. **Repeat signs**

The note E, and F in the middle register

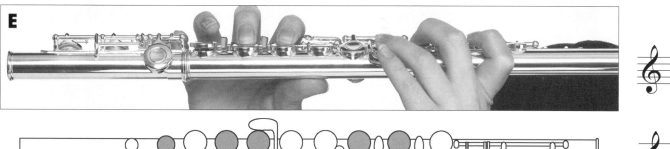

Exercise 1:

Compare the sounds of low E with the *higher* E and low F with the *higher* F.

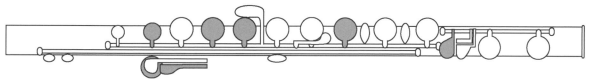

Exercise 2:

Awkward finger movements need lots of practice.

Try this many times every day, both tongued and slurred as shown.

The thick bar-lines with two dots tell you to **repeat** the music between them, in other words play *twice*.

Don't forget: your little finger is off for the D and back on for the E and F.

Exercise 3: the F major scale

This is the set of notes in the key of F major, ascending and descending by step.

21

Pieces for Lesson 5

25

Barcarolle

Offenbach

A new key for this piece.

Although you could play the lower part, the upper part would provide much better practice!

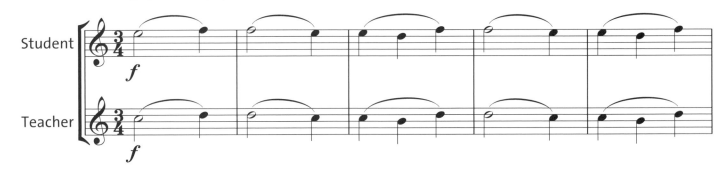

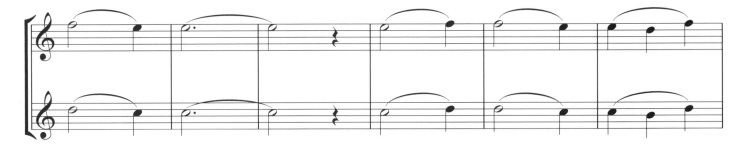

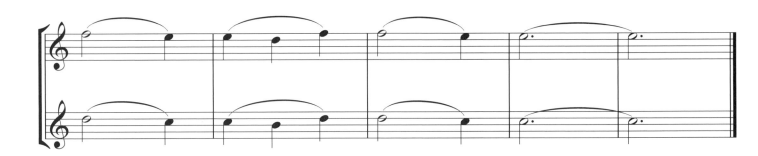

26

Abide With Me

Monk

Pieces for Lesson 5

Juggling

My Favorite Waltz

Pieces for Lesson 5

31–32 *Minuet*

THINK!

Don't be lazy with your tonguing –
proper articulation is essential
for a clear sound.

test: *for* Lessons 1 to 5

1. Note duration

On the staff below, draw notes of the indicated duration:

(4)

2. Rests

On the staff below, draw rests of the indicated duration:

(4)

3. Notes

On the staff below, draw the following notes as half notes:

G, **B**, **low E**, **C**, **high F**, **D** and **B♭**

(8)

4. Scales

Write out the F major scale including the key signature.

(2)

5. Bars

Draw barlines on this staff where they are needed.

(7)

Total **(25)**

goals:

1. **The note F sharp (F♯)**
2. **Octaves**

The note F♯

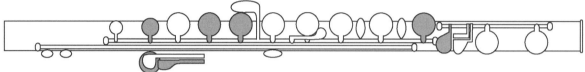

The sharp symbol (♯) raises the note to which it applies by a semitone.

This means that **F♯** is a semitone *above* **F** and a semitone *below* **G**.

Exercise 1:

Listen to how close F♯ and G sound

Exercise 2:

There is a tricky fingering change from E to F♯, and from D to F♯. This exercise needs to be practiced frequently.

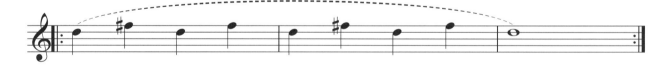

(Once a note is sharped, it remains so throughout the bar unless a natural sign is employed.)

Exercise 3: octave practice

Remember to adjust the embouchure.

26

Pieces for Lesson 6

Steal Away

Spiritual

Sea Song

Finger Blues

goals:

1. **The notes G (middle register) and low D**
2. **Common time**
3. **G major scale**

The notes G (middle register) and low D

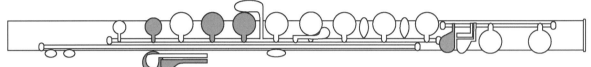

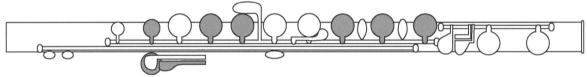

Exercise 1:

Practice makes perfect. Low notes can be a little tricky to play at first, but perseverance will be rewarded with a good, strong tone.

Work your way down to a low D, keeping your breath even.

Make sure your little finger stays firmly down until the moment you play the D.

Exercise 2:

Make sure you are breathing from your diaphragm for complete breath control, and experiment with your embouchure until these low notes come easily. And most important of all: relax!

Low notes can be hard to play with a strong tone. Ensure that your throat is open.

Imagine the shape of your throat when you steam up a window.

The large **C** at the beginning of this staff is shorthand for **common time,** which is the same as $\frac{4}{4}$.

Exercise 3:

G major scale and *arpeggio*.

Pieces for Lesson 7

O Come All Ye Faithful

Skye Boat Song

Scottish traditional

40–41

Repeat the section within the repeat signs, then go back to the beginning and play until the sign *Fine* (Italian for "end").

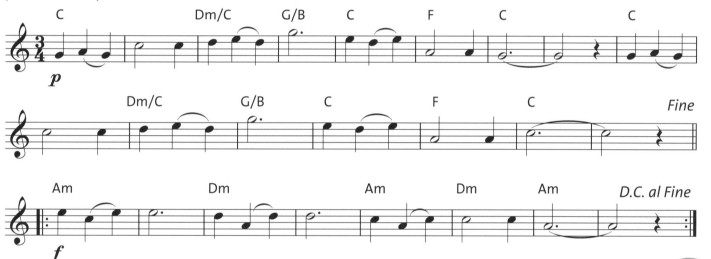

Scarborough Fair

English traditional

42

You could play the top part or the bottom part. If you feel ambitious, learn both!

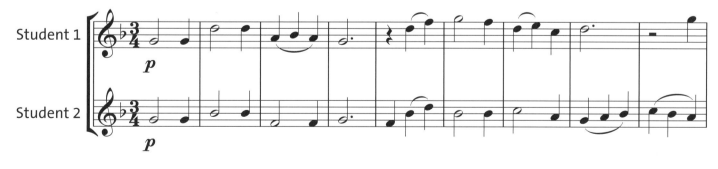

goals:

1. **The note C sharp (C♯)**
2. **Eighth notes**
3. **D major scale**
4. **Tempo and character markings**

The note C♯

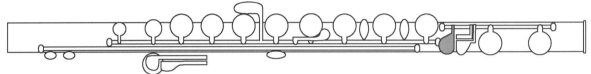

Exercise 1:
A tricky fingering change from C♯ to D.

Eighth notes

Single eighth notes and an eighth-note rest

So far you have studied and played notes that last for four beats (whole note), two beats (half note), and one beat (quarter note). You have also learned how to increase note durations by tying notes together or by adding a dot to a half note (for a three-beat note).

Eighths in pairs (worth one quarter per pair)

Eighth notes are notes which last for *half* the length of a quarter notes and should therefore be played *twice* as fast.

Exercise 2: *double or quit!*
Keep the beat steady and don't start too quickly.

Eighth notes as a group (a half note's worth)

Count: 1   2   3   4   1   2   3   4   1   2   3   4   1 & 2 & 3 & 4 &   1   2   3   4

Exercise 3: three beats per bar

Sight-reading (playing music that you haven't seen before) is an important skill for a musician.

Count: 1   2   3   1   2   3   1 & 2 & 3 &   1   2   3

Exercise 4: the scale of D major
Play this both slurred and tongued (as shown by the dotted slur lines).

Pieces for Lesson 8

Some short melodies for practice at playing eighth notes.

Yankee Doodle

This piece has only two beats per bar, and notice the tempo (speed) marking above the beginning of the piece.

Can Can

Offenbach

Nessun Dorma

Puccini

From The Magic Flute

Mozart

Swing Low, Sweet Chariot

Spiritual

goals:

1. **The note A in the middle register**
2. **Dotted quarter notes**

The note A in the middle register

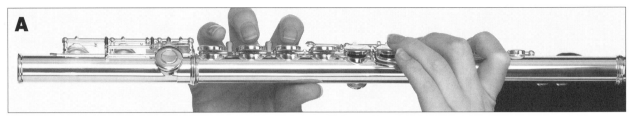

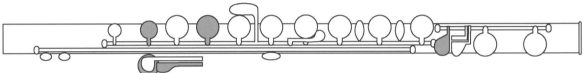

Exercise 1:

Play each note for as long as you can. Every time you practice you should start with long notes!

Exercise 2:

This is to help your control over octave leaps. Always aim for a clear sound in both the lower and middle register. Remember to adjust your embouchure rather than blowing harder. Play this slowly.

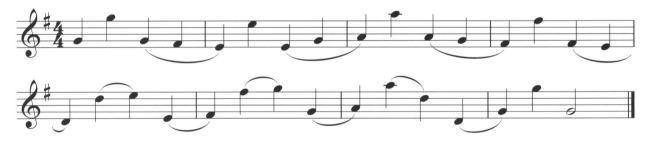

Dotted quarter notes

Dotted notes are often used instead of tying notes together: the fewer symbols there are on the page, the easier the music is to read.

As long ago as lesson 2 you discovered that a dot placed to the right of a half note increased its value from two beats to three. You could say that the dot *multiplies* its length by one and a half.

The same dot can be used to increase a quarter note's length from one beat to one and a half beats. In other words, instead of being the same length as two eighth notes tied together, its value is raised to three eighth notes.

Exercise 3:

Play this slowly so that you can count each eighth note. Learn to recognise the rhythms as you recognize words without really having to read them.

Count: **1   &   2   &   3   &   4   &   1   &   2   &   3   &   4   &   1...**

Exercise 4:

Play this exercise a few times, increasing the speed a little each time.

In time you should feel the rhythm and rely less on having to count each eighth note.

Exercise 5:

Because this type of rhythm is very common but a little tricky, here is another exercise.

This time there are three beats to a bar.

Pieces for Lesson 9

Auld Lang Syne

Sometimes a piece of music doesn't begin with a whole bar.

This piece begins with a single beat representing the last beat of a bar. This short bar (called an *upbeat* or *anacrusis*) is balanced by another short bar at the end. The two short bars add up to a whole bar.

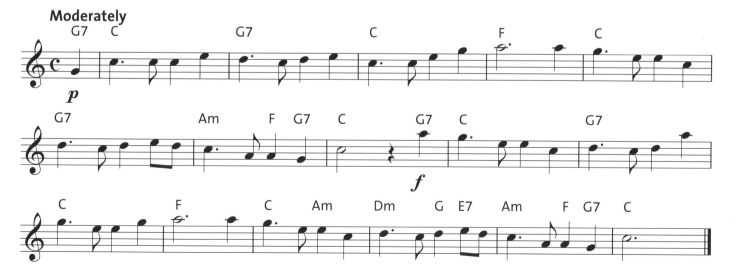

55

Allegro is the Italian word for "quick" and is very commonly seen as a tempo marking in music.

The top line here is the main tune, but you could also learn the bottom line for duet playing.

THINK!

Are you practicing properly?
Always start with long notes, making sure you are using your diaphragm and open throat. Stay relaxed when you play. Practice your exercises every day to build up embouchure strength. Don't be satisfied if a piece is nearly right.
It needs to be completely right before you should move on.

goals:

1. **Tone practice**
2. **More dynamics**

Practicing long notes *every day* is essential for developing a better sound.
Not only are you training your embouchure, diaphragm and throat, you are also building up vital muscle groups that improve your stamina and projection.

Exercise 1:
Use a full breath for each note. Rest between each one.

Exercise 2:
A clear tone in the middle register is hard to achieve. Aim to reduce the breath noise on all these notes.

Exercise 3:
Listen carefully to make sure that the lower register note is in tune with the middle register one,
and that they are at the same volume.

More dynamics

Only p and f have been introduced so far. These tell you to play either quietly or loudly. However, in between these extremes you could play *moderately quiet* or *moderately loud*. These are shown by the markings mp and mf. The m is short for *mezzo*, which is the Italian word for "half."

Exercise 4:
Play these notes with the dynamics indicated.

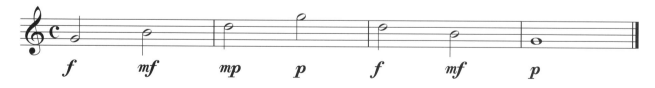

Pieces for Lesson 10

56-57 *Hark! The Herald Angels Sing*

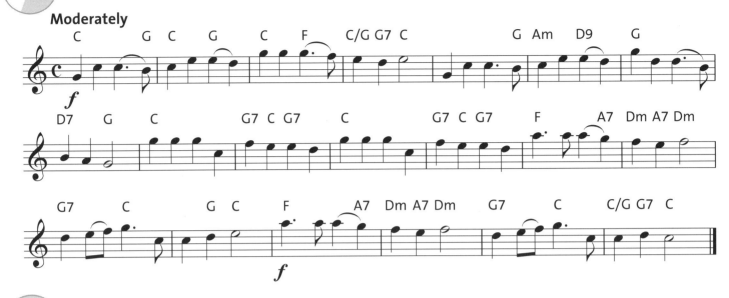

58-59 *Dixie*

Emmett

60 From *Symphony No.9* (play either part)

Beethoven

test: *for* Lessons 6 to 10

1. Note duration

On the staff below, draw notes of the indicated duration:

| 1 eighth note | 2 beats' worth of eighth notes | dotted quarter note | a note that lasts for 5 eighth notes |

(8)

2. Scale

On the staff below, draw the G major scale including the correct key signature:

(4)

3. Notes

On the staff below draw the following notes as quarter notes:

F♯, A, D (all middle register), and **low E**

(4)

4. Dynamics

What are the Italian words for:

Moderately loud _____

Moderately quiet _____

(4)

5. Naming ceremony

Identify all the items indicated by arrows.

Allegro

p

(5)

Total (25)

goals:

1. The notes E flat (E♭) and B flat (B♭)
2. The key of B♭ major

The notes E♭ and B♭

E♭

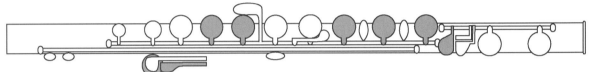

B♭

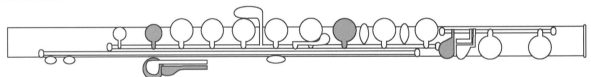

Exercise 1:

Make sure you change all the necessary fingers.

Remember to take your left index finger off for D and E♭ in the middle register.

Exercise 2: "the worm of misery"

In this exercise all notes are a semitone apart. This one will need a good deal of practice.

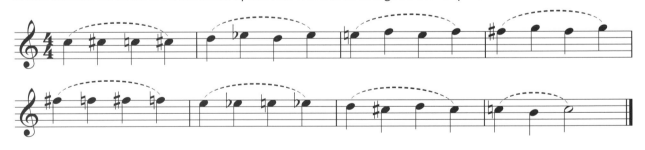

Exercise 3:

The scale and arpeggio of B♭ major. Remember what the key signature tells you.

Pieces for Lesson 11

Frère Jacques

French traditional

Up to four people can play this as a round. Begin when the previous instrument gets to the star in the third bar.

Romance No.1

Beethoven

Maintain a calm and steady tone throughout.

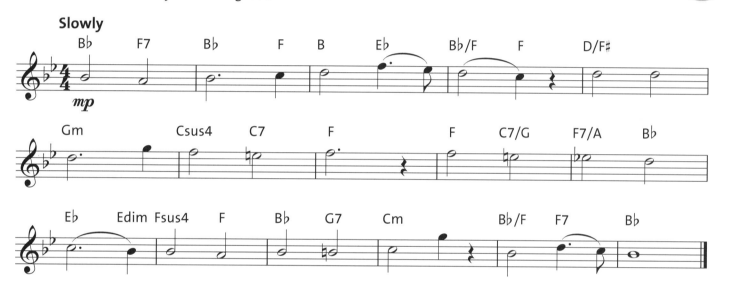

Can Can

Offenbach

Compare this version in F major with the one in G major in lesson 8.

goals:

1. **The notes B and C in the middle register**
2. **D.S. al Fine**

The notes B and C in the middle register

You might find that these high notes sound a little out of tune when you first play them. Keep a firm embouchure to ensure a steady tone and correct tuning.

B

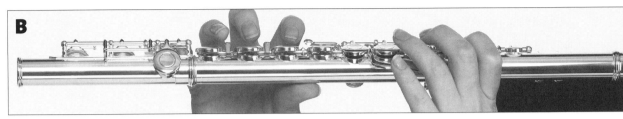

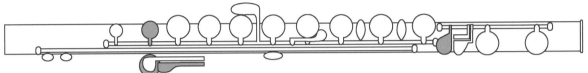

C

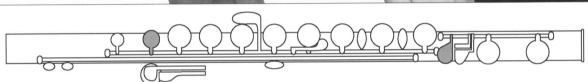

Exercise 1: long notes in the middle register

Exercise 2: octave slurs

This one needs regular practice.

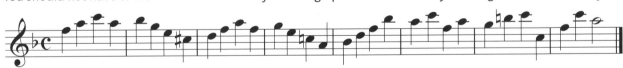

Exercise 3: recognizing higher notes

You should not have to work these notes out by counting upwards. Make sure you recognize them instantly.

Exercise 3: the C major scale and arpeggio

Pieces for Lesson 12

When The Saints Go Marching In

Play the section between the repeat bars twice. The first time, play the two bars at the end labeled 1, the second time play the bars labeled 2. These are called *first* and *second time endings*.

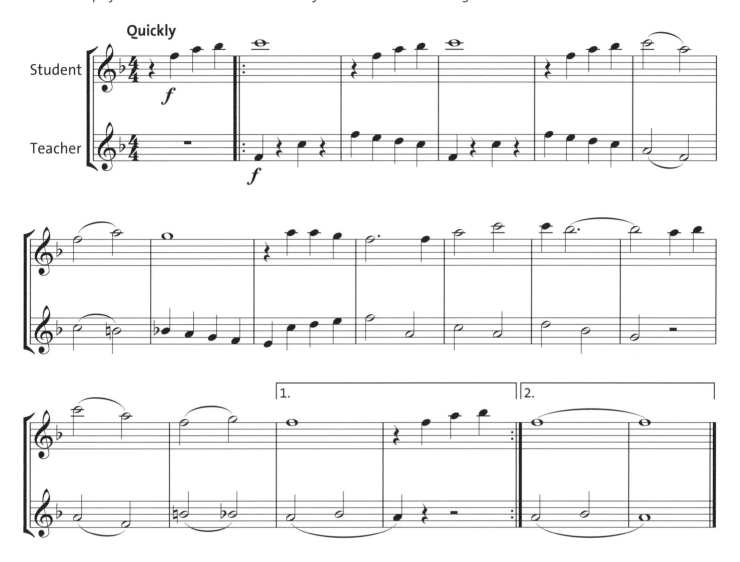

Reveille

Military traditional

D.S. al Fine means go back to the sign (𝄋) and play again until *Fine* (end).

goals:

1. **The note E flat (E♭) in the lower register**
2. **Finger dexterity**

The note E♭ in the lower register

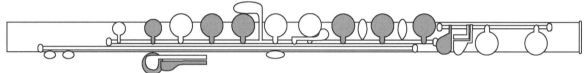

Fast fingers

This is the *don't run before you can walk* bit.

In order to play fast pieces, you must first spend time playing exercises and pieces slowly in order to gain complete control over every muscle that is being used.

Exercise 1:

Practice will help to build up "muscle memory": eventually you won't have to think about which fingers are required for a particular note, as your hands will "know" what to do.

This may seem easy, but aim for a perfect tone and precise finger movement.

Remember the fingering is different for the middle register D and E♭.

Exercise 2:

Coordinating your fingers can be hard. Be really critical of yourself; if it's not entirely perfect more practice is needed with both of these examples.

Exercise 3:

Play this many times to build up speed.

Pieces for Lesson 13

Camptown Races

Foster

Home On The Range

69-70

Danny Boy

Irish traditional

This is one of the most beautiful tunes ever written. Spend time on this to ensure complete fluency, control of dynamics and the correct slurs—it will be time well spent.

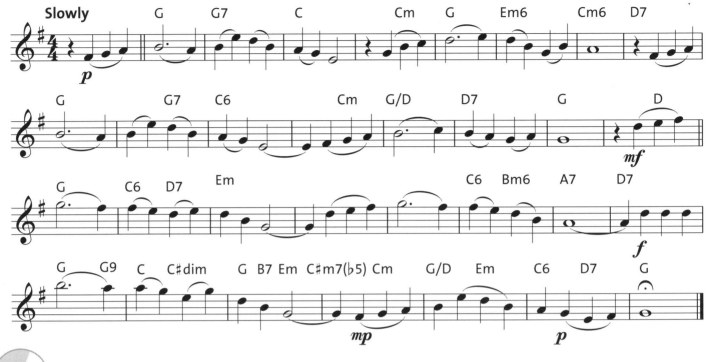

71

Swing Low, Sweet Chariot

Spiritual

goals:

1. **The note G sharp (G♯)**
2. **Minor keys and scales**

The note G♯

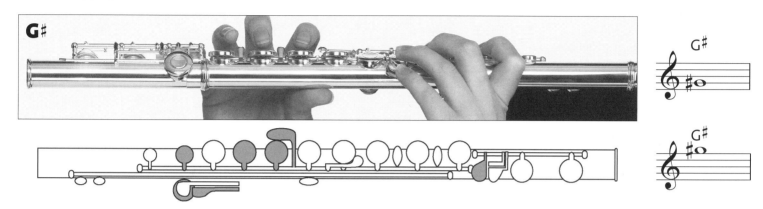

Exercise 1: low G, G♯ and A

This really works your little finger! Look out—the worms of misery are back!

Exercise 2:

The more you practice the G♯, the stronger your little finger will become, so here goes:

Exercise 3:

This is a Scottish folk song: play it vigorously.

Lesson 14

Major and minor

Most of the pieces you have played up to now have sounded cheerful. This is because they are virtually all in a *major* key, C major, F major, G major and so on. Sometimes, however, a composer wishes to express sadness in a piece. In general he or she will do this by writing the piece in a *minor* key.

Exercise 4: the A major scale

Play this a few times and listen to its bright character.

Exercise 5: A minor

The *key signature* is the same as C major, however look out for the G♯s, which are shown as they occur in the music (these are called **accidentals**).

Pieces for Lesson 14

Hava Nagila

Israeli traditional

A famous tune in a minor key (Dm). Start slowly and get faster as you go along.
This should sound very exciting!

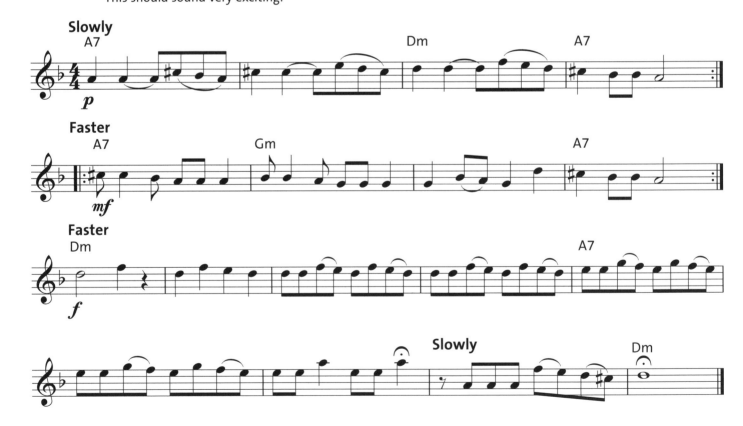

Pieces for Lesson 14

Go Down Moses

Spiritual

The melody is divided up among the three flutes, so they are all equally important.

Use the written dynamics to blend in when you are playing an accompanying line.

goals:

1. The notes C# and D in the upper register
2. Staccato and legato

The notes C# and D

C#

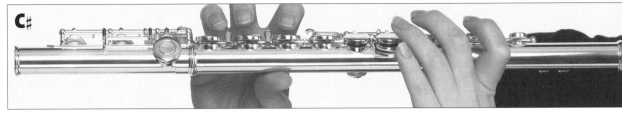

D

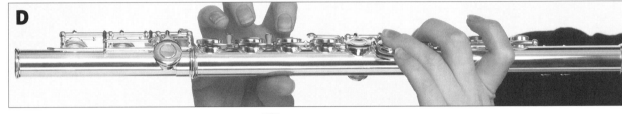

Exercise 1:

High notes only use a very short length of the instrument to make a sound. For this reason they need less breath for the same volume than a low note. Be careful not to use too much breath on high notes, otherwise it may affect the tone and the tuning — and your ears!

Match the tone and volumes of all of these notes.

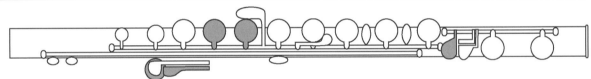

Exercise 2:

Play smoothly over these notes.

Exercise 3:

This is a two-octave D minor scale.

Staccato and legato

Legato means "joined up" and refers to notes that are slurred or tongued smoothly without a gap from the previous one. *Staccato* on the other hand means "detached." This is shown by a dot above or below the note:

Exercise 4:

Repeat this many times to achieve clear staccato tonguing.

Exercise 5:

Begin this very slowly otherwise the eighth notes will be too fast to tongue.

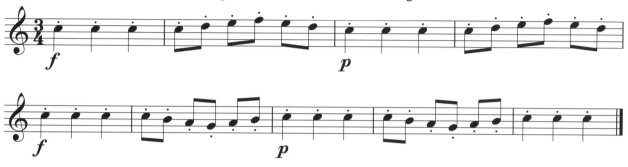

Pieces for Lesson 15

The Blue Danube Waltz

Johann Strauss II

Pieces for Lesson 15

76–77 *Oh! Susannah*
Stephen Foster

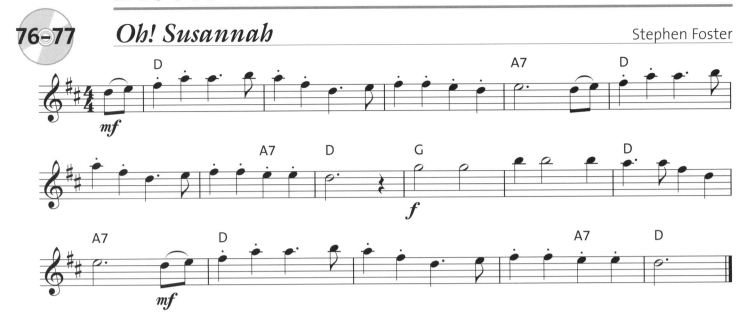

78–79 **Song Of The Volga Boatmen**
Russian traditional

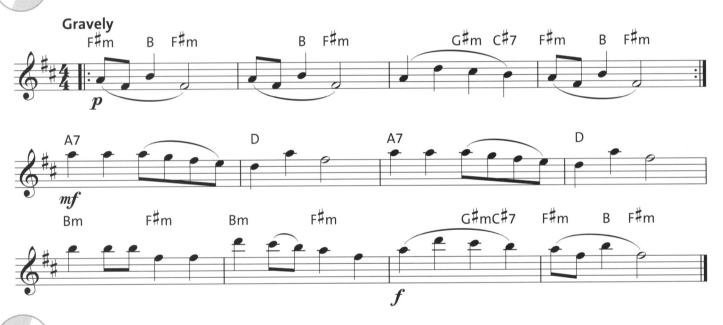

80–81 *Mango Walk*
Jamaican traditional

test: *for* Lessons 11 to 15

1. Key signatures

On the staff below, draw the correct key signatures for:

G major   F major   D minor   D major   C major

(5)

2. Dots

Simplify the music on the left using dots to get rid of the ties.

(5)

3. Notes

On the staff below draw the following notes as quarter notes:

Low register D and **G♯, middle register F♯, A, C♯,** and **top D**

(6)

4. Dynamics

What do the following words mean?

legato _____

staccato _____

(4)

5. Naming ceremony

Identify all the items indicated by arrows.

(5)

Total (25)

goals:

1. The notes C and C♯
2. Enharmonic notes

The notes C and C♯

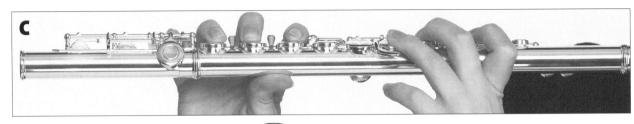

C

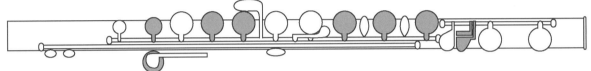

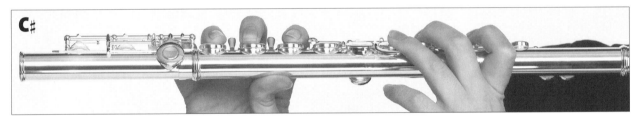

C♯

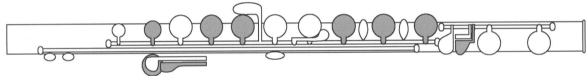

Exercise 1:

Compare the three E♭ notes in different octaves.

Play these long notes. Use a full breath for each one.

Don't forget, your little finger is needed for all the notes on a different key each time!

Try to keep the tone as similar as possible despite the big difference in pitch. They should all sound as though they are coming from the same instrument.

Enharmonic notes

From previous lessons, you know that A♭ is a semitone *below* A, and at the same time a semitone *above* G.

This means that the same note could be called G♯. These two notes are *enharmonic equivalents*.

Exercise 2:

These two short pieces need a note you have already learned, the first as a G♯, the second as an A♭.

Exercise 3:

Play the following notes. You *do* know the fingering for each one, however you may need to write down their enharmonic equivalents first.

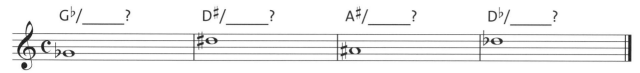

Gb/____?   D#/____?   A#/____?   Db/____?

Pieces for Lesson 16

The Entertainer

Scott Joplin

82

Enharmonic Blues

83–84

goals:

1. **Gradation of dynamics**
2. **More Italian terms**

Dynamic markings and tempo markings are very useful.

Music should always be expressive, and these markings will give a clue to the way a piece should be played.

All dynamic changes you have played so far have been instant. However, suddenly changing from *piano* to *forte* has a different impact from a gradual change.

Crescendo means gradually get louder, also shown as:

Diminuendo means gradually get quieter, also shown as:

Some other commonly used Italian words to describe a tempo are:

Allegro quickly   **Andante** at a walking pace   **Adagio** slowly

Rallentando (rall.) becoming slower   **Accelerando** (accel.) becoming faster

Pieces for Lesson 17   *Operatic Duets*

85

La Forza del Destino

Verdi

Hail The Conquering Hero (from *Judas Maccabeus*) — Handel

William Tell Overture — Rossini

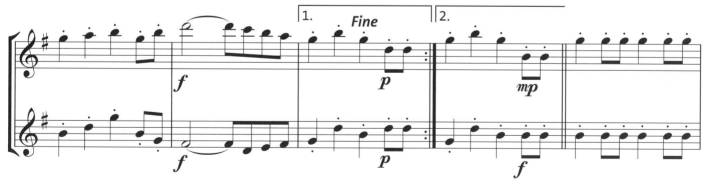

goals:

1. **Swing eights**
2. **Playing jazz pieces**

Swing

Remember not to play the eighths too "straight," but instead give them a healthy bounce.

You might imagine the beat divided into three, with the first two-thirds for the first eighth and the final third for the second eighth.

In classical music all eighth notes are played exactly as written, that is, lasting half as long as a quarter note.

In jazz, however, eighth notes are normally played unevenly, with the first of each pair longer than half a beat, and the second shorter to compensate. This is called **swing**.

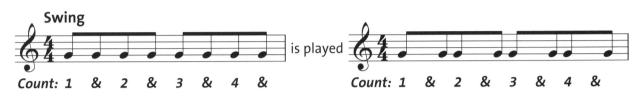

Exercise 1:

Play this E minor scale in swing rhythm. Try it first all tongued, then with the slurs as written.

Pieces for Lesson 18

88-89 *Little Brown Jug*

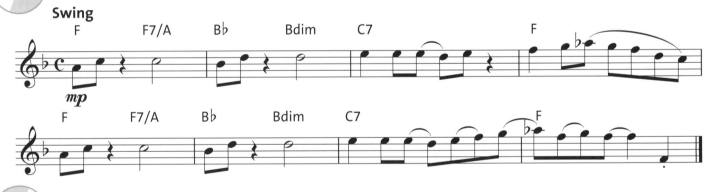

90-91 *Joshua Jazz*

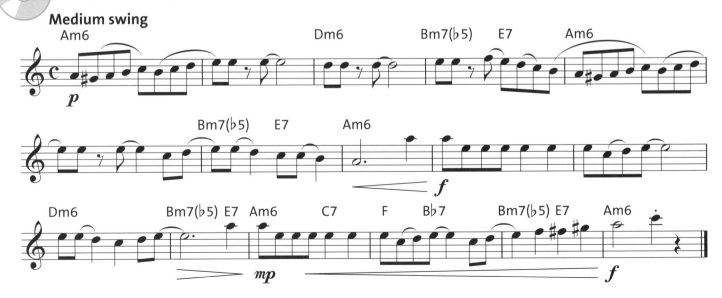

Pieces for Lesson 18

Maryland, My Maryland

Moderate swing

goals:

1. **Good technique through scale practice**
2. **Ensemble playing**

Practicing

Practising scales every day will help you to:

- Train your fingers to respond quickly in various keys
- Ensure evenness in the timing of notes
- Develop a consistent tone over the instrument's range
- Increase control over your breathing
- Improve your listening awareness of note relationships

The following scales and arpeggios are recommended practice for flautists at a relatively early stage. They should be practiced both slurred and tongued.

F major

G major

D major (two octaves)

E minor

A minor

Pieces for Lesson 19

Gypsy Rover

Pieces for Lesson 19

Down By The Riverside

Lively swing

goals:

1. $\frac{6}{8}$ **time signature (compound time)**
2. Traditional-style songs in $\frac{6}{8}$ time

Simple and compound time

$\frac{2}{4}$, $\frac{3}{4}$, and $\frac{4}{4}$ are all *simple* time signatures.

The top number tells you how many beats per bar, and the bottom number tells you that each beat
is worth one quarter note. This also means that each beat can be divided into **two** eighth notes.

Exercise 1: counting in simple time

Count: 1   2   3   4   1   &   2   &   3   &   4   &   1...

In *compound* time, however, each beat is worth **three** eighth notes.
This means that each beat must now be a *dotted* quarter notes.

Exercise 2: counting in compound time

Count: 1 & a 2 & a   1   &   a   2   &   a   1   2

Exercise 3:

Here's a well-known tune in $\frac{6}{8}$ time. Remember to think in *two*.

Count: 1 & a 2 & a   1 & a   2 & a   1 & a   2 & a   1...

Irish jigs are in $\frac{6}{8}$ time, as is the well-known "We're Off To See The Wizard" from The Wizard Of Oz. $\frac{6}{8}$ pieces are often lively. Counting two groups of three is much easier than trying to count all six eighth notes.

THINK!

Remember to keep a steady beat.
You might want to use a metronome.
Some people like to tap their foot
when they play, but this takes a little
practice before it comes naturally.

Lesson 20

Pieces for Lesson 20

93 *The Animals Went In Two By Two* Traditional

 94-95 *For He's A Jolly Good Fellow* Traditional

1. Enharmonic

Rewrite the following notes as their enharmonic equivalents:

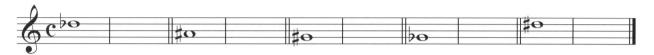

(5)

2. Afraid of heights?

Write the following music one octave higher:

(6)

3. Breath control

Play this note with a steady tone, controlling your breath at all times.

You will score one point (up to a maximum of five) for every three seconds held.

(5)

4. Expression

Write the Italian words for:

Get louder _____   Get quieter _____

Get quicker _____   Get slower _____

(4)

5. Scale test

Play the following from memory:

1. E minor scale

2. D major arpeggio

3. F major scale

4. G major arpeggio

5. A minor scale

(5)

Total (25)

CD backing tracks

1 Tuning track
2 Virtuoso Performance
3 Valley Song
4 Going Cuckoo
5 Au Clair de la Lune *demonstration*
6 Au Clair de la Lune *backing only*
7 Back To Bed *demonstration*
8 Back To Bed *backing only*
9 Grumpy Graham
10 Medieval Dance
11 Barcarolle
12 Jingle Bells *demonstration*
13 Jingle Bells *backing only*
14 Largo from New World Symphony *demonstration*
15 Largo from New World Symphony *backing only*
16 Lightly Row
17 Knight Time *demonstration*
18 Knight Time *backing only*
19 When The Saints Go Marching In *demonstration*
20 When The Saints Go Marching In *backing only*
21 Joshua Fought The Battle Of Jericho *demonstration*
22 Joshua Fought The Battle Of Jericho *backing only*
23 Coventry Carol *demonstration*
24 Coventry Carol *backing only*
25 Barcarolle
26 Abide With Me
27 Juggling *demonstration*
28 Juggling *backing only*
29 My Favorite Waltz *demonstration*
30 My Favorite Waltz *backing only*
31 Minuet *demonstration*
32 Minuet *backing only*
33 Steal Away *demonstration*
34 Steal Away *backing only*
35 Sea Song

36 Finger Blues *demonstration*
37 Finger Blues *backing only*
38 O Come All Ye Faithful *demonstration*
39 O Come All Ye Faithful *backing only*
40 Skye Boat Song *demonstration*
41 Skye Boat Song *backing only*
42 Scarborough Fair
43 Yankee Doodle *demonstration*
44 Yankee Doodle *backing only*
45 Can Can *demonstration*
46 Can Can *backing only*
47 Nessun Dorma *demonstration*
48 Nessun Dorma *backing only*
49 Magic Flute *demonstration*
50 Magic Flute *backing only*
51 Swing Low, Sweet Chariot *demonstration*
52 Swing Low, Sweet Chariot *backing only*
53 Auld Lang Syne *demonstration*
54 Auld Lang Syne *backing only*
55 Allegro from *Spring*
56 Hark! The Herald Angels Sing *demonstration*
57 Hark! The Herald Angels Sing *backing only*
58 Dixie *demonstration*
59 Dixie *backing only*
60 from *Symphony No. 9*
61 Romance No.1 *demonstration*
62 Romance No.1 *backing only*
63 Can Can *demonstration*
64 Can Can *backing only*
65 When The Saints Go Marching In
66 Camptown Races
67 Home On The Range *demonstration*
68 Home On The Range *backing only*
69 Danny Boy *demonstration*
70 Danny Boy *backing only*
71 Swing Low, Sweet Chariot

72 Hava Nagila *demonstration*
73 Hava Nagila *backing only*
74 The Blue Danube *demonstration*
75 The Blue Danube *backing only*
76 Oh! Susannah *demonstration*
77 Oh! Susannah *backing only*
78 Song Of The Volga Boatmen *demonstration*
79 Song Of The Volga Boatmen *backing only*
80 Mango Walk *demonstration*
81 Mango Walk *backing only*
82 The Entertainer
83 Enharmonic Blues *demonstration*
84 Enharmonic Blues *backing only*
85 La Forza del Destino
86 Hail The Conquering Hero
87 William Tell Overture
88 Little Brown Jug *demonstration*
89 Little Brown Jug *backing only*
90 Joshua Jazz *demonstration*
91 Joshua Jazz *backing only*
92 Maryland, My Maryland
93 The Animals Went In Two By Two
94 For He's A Jolly Good Fellow *demonstration*
95 For He's A Jolly Good Fellow *backing only*

How to use the CD

The tuning note on track 1 is an A.

After track 2, which gives an idea of how the flute can sound, the backing tracks are listed in the order in which they appear in the book. Look for the symbol 🔘 in the book for the relevant backing track.

Where both parts of a duet are included on the CD, the top part is in one channel and the bottom part is in the other channel.